We Will Follow

Our Family's Journey from Obedience to Faith

KELLY R. HENLEY

WESTBOW
PRESS®
A DIVISION OF THOMAS NELSON
& ZONDERVAN

WestBow Press books may be ordered through booksellers or by contacting:

WestBow Press
A Division of Thomas Nelson & Zondervan
1663 Liberty Drive
Bloomington, IN 47403
www.westbowpress.com
1 (866) 928-1240

ISBN: 978-1-9736-7958-5 (sc)
ISBN: 978-1-9736-7960-8 (hc)
ISBN: 978-1-9736-7959-2 (e)

Library of Congress Control Number: 2019918214

Print information available on the last page.

WestBow Press rev. date: 11/22/2019

Introduction

By the word of our testimony we can triumph over the enemy. We also have the ability to help those in our circle of influence. The people that have been placed purposefully around you are your circle. Sometimes all it takes to lift someone up is to help them see that they are not alone.

We all struggle. We all need encouragement. The world is full of people pretending they have it all together. I am here to tell you that I do not. I am even a Christian and I don't have it all together. The world likes to pretend Christians have it all figured out but I assure you, we don't. We just know the one that does and try to live by His example.

In this book you will find my unique, honest, and non churchy perspective as I share our family's story. I have included our many struggles and victories. As you read our story I pray you are encouraged. I pray you see through the struggles and see the purpose in them. I pray you see that in this life you can have great joy, peace, and comfort even through the struggles. You were created for a purpose, yes you. You were created to do good works. There is a plan for you and it's a good one.

Revelation 12:11 They triumphed over him
by the blood of the Lamb and by the word
of their testimony;

Chapter 1

Our control over our circumstances had been taken, again. It was clear that God was in control. I had tried my best to take the reins. I had tried to rally all my little Christian friends to support my will. I had rebuked "Satan" not to mess up my plans. I had cried, pleaded, and begged. And guess what? God was still in control.

One thing I had control over was how I responded to my circumstances. Would I handle this gracefully or like a blubbering idiot? The facts were scary. I needed to find God's truth.

How quickly I had forgotten what God had said when I had taken my eyes off of Him. At this point I wasn't believing He was behind us. Maybe others were right. Maybe we were just irresponsible new Christians thinking we heard God.

Let me back up a couple years so you can understand what's going on. My name is Kelly and my husband's name is David, but we call him Bubba. We grew up in different parts of the country. He grew up in eastern North Carolina on the Outer Banks. Majority of his life, along with generations before him, home was that beach. He attended church as a boy, before falling away for many years. I grew up in rural New York, having practically no knowledge of who Jesus was or anything to do with the church. My family moved to the beach when I was fifteen years old.

We spent most of our teen years in rebellion for our own reasons. Our paths crossing briefly along the way. At age twenty one our paths would cross at just the right time. At this time he was a single father with a beautiful two year old little girl, Nadia.

We fell in love. Less than a year later we were married. Finding out shortly after we were expecting our son, David. I'll try my best to explain a bit of the effect finding out we were expecting had on me. I feel it's worth explaining in case someone else has felt the same way. Sometimes just knowing we aren't alone makes a big difference.

Up until this point in my life I had been around and helped care for others' kids including nieces and nephews. Caring for them as I thought I would my own children one day. We were intentionally trying to get pregnant. I should not have been shocked when we conceived. Yet I was. The day I realized I was expecting my entire world changed. Not in a cliché greatest thing that's ever happened to me kind of way.

I locked myself in the bathroom. Refusing to come out. The entire world, including my husband, suddenly seemed dangerous to me. The only job I had was to protect that baby. In that moment I experienced my first taste of unconditional love and I couldn't handle it. I spent the next two years in therapy trying to work through my feelings. Clearly it was an irrational reaction to a natural feeling.

After David was born we decided it would be best if I stayed home with the kids. Instead of going back to work. Ok, it was really my idea but Bubba agreed.

Staying with the kids was exactly what I wanted to do. Yet the most isolating thing I had ever done. I still felt alone even though we were very active and constantly out doing things. It was the most confusing feeling ever since I was never actually alone because of the kids. Though I always felt alone due to the lack of adult interaction.

We decided to begin homeschooling after Nadia finished the second grade. It was the best decision for her at the time. Although this would be even more isolating for me. Most of my socializing with other moms had taken place at the school.

I noticed all my need for attention being projected on Bubba. I began to need him to be everything for me. My entire social circle was now put on his shoulders. This was a recipe for disaster. At the end of each day leaving him feeling pressured to fill all these shoes while I was left frustrated because he couldn't.

On one particularly lonely day someone knocked on our door. Standing on the porch were two ladies about my age. They wanted to talk to me. I desperately needed someone to talk to. She told me they were Jehovah's Witnesses. I had no idea what that meant, but ok. I was honestly so desperate to talk to another adult I didn't even care who they were or why they were at my house.

She had a Bible. I had never opened one, let alone read one. It didn't matter to me what she wanted to talk about. The fact she wanted to talk to me was good enough. I'm not even sure I listened to anything she said. Instead, I just talked about random mom stuff for an hour. Complaining about chores, kids not listening, and the struggles of being new to home schooling.

One of the ladies home schooled. She told me about different home school groups in the area. This seemed like such an amazing coincidence. Back when I used to think life was just random chance. At the end of our conversation she asked if I wanted them to come back. Yes! Are you kidding me? Of course I did. I finally had friends.

I was actually shocked when they came back. I hadn't really expected them to. I had pretty much ignored them. Rambling about my own circumstances. I was determined to at least pretend I was listening this time.

Each week she wanted to talk about the Bible and I just wanted to talk about me. She listened to me and I began to listen to her. She would explain to me what the Bible was. How it had become the Bible. Every time I talked to her about a problem I was having she would ask if she could pray about it. Explaining to me why she prays. That prayer was a way that she talked to God. She always asked if I wanted her to come back and I did. I waited all week for her to return.

Each week she brought different ladies. They were all genuine, kind, and interested in our family. I knew without a doubt they cared about us. They cared about me. I wasn't sure where she was finding all these ladies but it was great. I wasn't lonely anymore.

We tried one of the home school groups and absolutely loved it. If you home school or stay at home I strongly encourage you to research groups in your area. Our husbands are not meant to be our entire social circles.

I would learn this group was a Christian home school group. I had even signed a statement of faith. Treating it like any other contract I had not read before signing. I would not have joined had I read it. I was not a Christian. I may have learned through the ladies at the house that they and others believed there was a God. But I was not so sure myself.

Luke 19:10 For the Son of Man came to seek and save those who are lost. NLT

Chapter 2

Over time I began to realize based on the evidence they showed me and the information in that Bible that God was real. With her I could question everything. If she didn't have the answer she would find it and get back to me the next week.

Some concepts were hard to understand like. Why Jesus would die for us? Why would He do that if we were the bad ones and He was so perfect? Why would God make Him do that if God were so good? A lot of it made no sense to me.

She explained week after week that because God loved all people He had sent His only son (Jesus) to be the ransom for us. She explained that she used the word "ransom" because it was a debt that had been paid in exchange for something else. That "something else" was our restored relationship to God. Which had been messed up because of the sin (bad stuff) all people are guilty of.

I questioned everything they said. The information in the Bible was matching up with literal points in history. It was all pointing to the fact that someone actually created everything, including me.

I had to make a choice to believe them or to continue believing that life was all just random coincidence. That I was here by mistake. Continue believing there was no order or meaning to anything in the world. That we are supposed to try and make the best out of a life in a messed-up world until we all died. Their explanation was profoundly less depressing.

If I chose to believe the Bible was true than I'm pretty sure that makes the Bible the instruction book for life. I had always been told there wasn't one. Maybe they just didn't know about it. Some Bibles even have an index that could point me to the scriptures that would help with specific topics like fear, anxiety, and sadness. Along with many other topics.

At this point I believed there was a God. Believing someone exists is a far cry from trusting them. There were two very big details about God I just wasn't understanding. How He allows things to happen? How could I ever call him my father?

My father passed away two months before I was born. He'd been struck by a car while crossing the street. I spent my entire life angry. Blaming everyone for his death. Finding out there was a creator of the universe just chilling up in Heaven that could have done something to prevent me from growing up without a father. That was not sitting well with me. I remember vividly thinking, "You tell me a reason that is good enough for a girl to grow up never even meeting her father."

We would spend week after week going over this. Would I believe them? Or would I allow this to make me push away everything else she had to offer. I knew I had a choice to accept everything in that book or nothing.

Each week we would go through scriptures. Romans 8:28 And we know that in all things God works for the good of those who love him. Genesis 50:20 But as for you, you meant evil against me; but God meant it for good NKJV.

One scripture that I would not understand until I was living it. This scripture would show me that God allowed what happened to me for a very special and important reason. 2 Corinthians 1:4 Who comforts us in all our troubles, so that we can comfort those in any trouble with the comfort we ourselves receive from God.

Around this time Nadia would lose her Nana to cancer. All those years of hating and blaming everyone for the death of my father gave me the experience and strength I would need to pull her out of the same destructive patterns. I could recognize the desire in her to push everyone away. Trying to make them feel as she felt inside. I could recognize it because I had lived it my entire life.

Romans 10:17 So, faith comes from hearing, that is, hearing the Good News about Christ. NLT

Chapter 3

At the home school group one of the moms invited us to her church for a dinner. She explained that it was free, and all were welcome. After the dinner the kids would have activities with their peers. This was exactly what I had been looking for. I had been concerned about the kids not having enough structure once we started home schooling.

Could all that really be free? Free to anyone? Who just feeds random people they don't know and has kids' activities every week for free?

Apparently the church does. We went and to my surprise it was free. It was amazing. The kids and I both loved it. Everyone was kind and welcoming. Just like the ladies at the house and the home school group. There was this whole world of nice people that I never knew existed. Now I never wanted to live without them. How had I made it this far in life not knowing there was so much kindness in the world?

Just the kids and I went to the Wednesday night dinners at first. To Bubba it may have seemed like a play date I was taking the kids to.

Bubba was invited by a co-worker to attend his church's Friday night service. I was on a girl scouting camping trip with Nadia that weekend so him and David went. They enjoyed it and decided to go back the following Sunday.

Let me paint you a picture of what our lives looked like for almost a year. Sundays were spent at Liberty Christian Fellowship, a non-denominational church. Wednesday nights the kids and I attended Kitty Hawk Baptist Church for dinners and Bible study. Once a week Bible studies with the Jehovah's Witnesses and co-op with the Christian home school group. Jesus was everywhere and we couldn't get enough.

I faintly remember the reactions of people as I nonchalantly described the fact my family was not only involved in multiple churches but totally different denominations. To me this was completely normal. I didn't have any preconceived Christian norms.

In all honesty I was testing God. I didn't understand why there were different denominations and translations. I was still a bit skeptical of why these people were all so nice. Maybe that was the New Yorker in me or maybe I had been hurt one too many times to just trust people.

While studying with the Jehovah's Witnesses I would have different Bible translations to compare scriptures. Questioning why there were so many translations if they all pretty much said the same thing. She never seemed to be offended by my constant questioning. She cared about me and I knew that. Her love for me was a big part of why I kept seeking the answers. I researched and researched what was said at different groups or churches. Trying to see through opinions to find the facts.

I heard about a Mom's Group through Liberty and decided to give it a try. I'll never forget that first day sitting in that room with those moms as they shared their struggles with loneliness and isolation while staying home with their kids. I wasn't the only mom struggling to balance the feelings of gratefulness with loneliness while being able to stay home.

On that day I started to realize the importance of being transparent about my struggles. The world is full of people so afraid to share their struggles for fear of looking weak. For fear of being the only one who's going through that particular struggle. I realized on that day how much freedom I felt by simply hearing others publicly professing their struggles. I knew I wanted to help others not feel alone.

In Mom's Group we discussed a scripture that would change the way I saw myself. This scripture would speak to my heart and soul everything I had ever longed to hear. Psalm 139:13-14 for you created my inmost being; you knit me together in my mother's womb. I praise you because I am fearfully and wonderfully made; your works are wonderful; I know that full well.

No one had ever told me I was a mistake although I felt that way. I had spent much of my childhood hating everyone and everything. Assuming the world felt the same way about me. To read in this book that the creator of the universe had personally formed me, meant I was planned for. I was wanted. I wasn't a mistake.

The other verses in the chapter go on to explain that He sees me. Not the side of me I pretend to be but the real me. The side of me I felt wasn't good enough. The parts of my personality I always tried to cover up and hide. All along He had seen me and chose me anyway. He chose to send Jesus to die on that cross for me.

At the end of this book I have included all of Psalm 139. I encourage you to just read it. It's talking about you and me. Not just the churchy have it all together type of people.

We were planned for. We are seen. Even though He sees our mess He continues to choose us anyway.

One Sunday morning at Liberty the pastor was preaching on independence. How we needed to give up our desire to be independent for God to work in our lives. I understood the message at this point. I understood who Jesus was and what He wanted for all people. I understood what He had done for us. Would I give up control of our lives and give over control to Him? Giving up control contradicted everything I had been taught in the world. The world had taught me to be strong. Handle things myself. The more independent you are the better. This meant giving up all control. Making the choice to not be independent.

I had engulfed us in all activities Jesus related through the churches, Bible studies, and home school groups. I was beginning to realize it was all the equivalent of a very good hobby. The pastor was referring to more. It was about giving everything to God. Giving Him our whole lives, family, and desires.

This God that I now knew existed did not just want my Sunday mornings and my Wednesday nights. It wasn't enough that I listened to Christian music, watched Christian movies, and read Christian books. He wanted all of me. He wanted our lives. Most of all our hearts. We were still living for us while we were enjoying our cool new Jesus hobby.

That Sunday as Bubba and I left our seats to walk to the front of that church, we gave up our independence. We gave over our lives to God. We were letting go of our control and giving it over to Him. On that day our lives, family, and marriage began to change. What had once been a bunch of Jesus activities began to feed our souls. Began to give our life new meaning. The things we were doing didn't change that much but the reasons we were doing them completely changed.

My lack of awareness that I needed a savior and His church did not change the fact that I needed them. Or the fact that He pursued me anyway. Pursued me even through my unbelief and my doubts. He used my loneliness to draw me to Him.

God would eventually direct me to stop the weekly studies with the Jehovah Witnesses. It was one of the hardest things I had ever done. I truly believe we wouldn't be where we are today without God using them. God would also direct our family to the Baptist church as our home church. We needed the closeness of a small church family. A place to learn, grow, and be mentored.

Many people at these churches played a huge role in our walk. Coming along side of us to pray for us, giving us guidance, and most of all loving our little family. I continued attending Mom's Group. I needed them and I praise God He let me continue.

I cherish the fact that my walk started with so many denominations and translations. We were brought to Jesus through unity. We the people are the church not the buildings. The same love of Jesus was shown to us through each church.

The churches working together has instilled in me a desire to be involved in multiple churches. A need to remember the church is not confined to their own building or even their own denomination. The church is the people in those buildings. We should remember all we need to have in common is Jesus. Because He is all that matters. As you seek His guidance He will lead you in the right direction.

In our case I truly believe that one church alone could not have brought us to the knowledge of Jesus as our savior. Through them working together our family was saved. For that I will forever be grateful. They all continued to walk with our family as we grew in our faith. They were always available to pray and encourage us.

Matthew 7:21 Not everyone who says to me, 'Lord, Lord,' will enter the kingdom of heaven, but only the one who does the will of my Father who is in heaven.

Chapter 4

Before long we began to feel a sort of disconnect from the beach. We struggled to understand what this meant. Were we experiencing what the Bible says in Hebrews? That this world is not our home. Maybe we were just looking forward to things yet to come. Were we just not content with our lives?

As we continued to learn more about God through the church and Bible studies we realized for us this was more. As we sought God about these feelings it was clear the beach would not be our home forever. The only question was when He would tell us to leave.

We were on fire for God. All we wanted to do was go and go now. We felt there was so much more for us to do out in the world. A life we couldn't wait to get started on. He was holding us back. We didn't understand why. We thought we were ready.

In our waiting we started to learn that God has a perfect time and season for everything. His timing is not the same as our timing. Until He said to go we would stay right where we were. Trying to be a blessing to the people around us the best we knew how.

Of course we messed up and made mistakes. We learned how to handle certain situations better. How to handle people better. He placed people in our lives to feed into us exactly what we needed; when we needed it. He gave us a safe place to grow and mess up. Always giving us the chance to learn from our mistakes.

He put above us a pastor and leadership that would allow us to try new things. Where we lacked experience, we had enthusiasm.

Each season we tried serving in different areas from children's ministry to outreach. Trying to see which area God was calling us to.

A woman speaking at a Bible study I attended had just returned from Africa. They were calling her a missionary. I asked her that night what a missionary was. She explained that she had lived in Africa for four years. Sharing Jesus with the native people.

Bubba and I would marvel at the fact people literally got to travel around and tell people about Jesus. We started to pray, pretty much beg, that God would allow us to do this. We started seeing videos of church planters and missionaries during the church services. As the video would play my heart would start to beat so fast. I'd almost have a hard time catching my breath.

We prayed and waited for our church to announce they were going on a mission trip. We were definitely going on the next one. We felt led to ask the head of our WMU® for information. This group had missions in the name. Surely, she could help or at least point us in the direction we needed to start looking. There had to be some ten-step program to becoming a missionary.

We would do it. Starting now! Clearly, we lacked patience. We went to her and asked, "How do we go on a mission trip?" She replied, "You pray about it, pick one, and go."

What? We can just go. We didn't have to wait for the church to go on one? No way could it be that easy. Didn't we need to be qualified? Didn't we need to be Christians longer?

Obviously, we were the only ones thinking we weren't qualified. We were also the only ones not aware that the reason we felt this way about missions was because God was calling us to missions. Plus, others knew God would equip us if He had called us. So technically we didn't need to be qualified because He already was.

She directed us to the WMU® website. That night we prayed and looked through the trips coming up. The Colorado trip was the only one that allowed for the kids to go.

Sure it was far away but we had driven through Colorado on

our cross country trip for my brother's wedding. On that trip we realized our family loved two things, Jesus and traveling. The next day at church she had the same papers about Colorado to show us. We took that as another confirmation. We were going on our first mission trip!

In the months leading up to that trip we grew. Learning so much about us and God's character. Helping us to realize on our own we are stubborn, prideful, and arrogant. With Jesus, we can be willing, meek, and humble. Since we allowed him to change and mold us during this process He was able to teach us through each mistake. We sure did make a lot of mistakes.

We were the only people going on this mission trip from our church. That terrified me. I really wanted to just go along with a group and have others be in charge. We would be "in charge" of our first mission trip.

The church would help direct us. At times not helping as much as I thought they should. Only to realize this was all God's plan. I had expected the church to do everything since they knew more. But we needed to rely on God through this. Not the others' experience at the church. We needed to get our own experience. We needed to make mistakes in order to know how not to do it next time. Had the church done what I thought they should, we would not have learned the lessons we needed to. The lessons that would later serve us well.

One of our big hurdles was fundraising. Pastor more than suggested that we needed to send out letters to everyone we knew. Asking for help in monetary support and prayers. This seemed like a horrible idea. Most of the people we knew weren't even Christians. I was nervous about what they would think. Some of these people knew our past. Would they believe we were different? Not just that but we were not the type of people to ask for help from anyone.

Although we thought this was a bad idea, we did it anyway. Aware that Pastor knew way more about this kind of stuff than we did. Through sending out the letters and asking for support we learned how to accept help, to value prayers, and to be confident in who we were in Jesus. Grasping the idea of sharing the blessing with others. Learning that some are called to go while others are called to send.

I'll never forget the morning Pastor came up to me and asked which Sunday would work for me to go up and address the church about the trip. I literally laughed in his face. "None," I answered. "There is not going to be a Sunday that will work. Because there is no way I am getting up in front of that church and talking about anything. You are crazy!" Thankfully I only thought that second part.

Pastor never seemed to be rattled by my inability to speak to him the way someone should a pastor. He calmly gave me the dates I had to choose from and walked away. I'll never know if he walked away from our many exchanges laughing to himself at my immaturity or irritated at my rudeness.

It didn't usually take God long to get a hold of my little immature self. I'm pretty sure by the end of the day we had chosen a date. I'll never forget how nervous I was standing in front of that church. How sick I felt. Or that I used the phrase, "I feel like I'm going to throw up," in front of the whole congregation.

During this process we learned that the church supported us. They didn't just support what we were doing, they supported us. They thought we were capable of doing this. Giving us the confidence we needed to continue.

Romans 10:15 And how can anyone preach unless they are sent? As it is written: "How beautiful are the feet of those who bring good news!"

Chapter 5

We started our adventure driving the five days to Colorado. As we were heading over the bridge to leave the beach I received a text, "You are a missionary now." The text was from the missionary at Bible study. She was right. We are missionaries! Wasn't long ago when we hadn't even known what a missionary was. That's how awesome God is! If we are willing. He will use us.

I'm going to take a break from our journey real quick to point out an important lesson. One that I don't want you to miss. The years I have been a Christian at this point are way less than the amount of years I spent lost. I mean twenty seven lost and three saved. The amount of years the enemy spent tearing me down were no match for what Jesus could do in such a short amount of time. It doesn't matter how many years you've spent lost. Doesn't matter how many lies you've believed. If you give Jesus an honest shot to help you. I promise you, you will be shocked at how fast He can completely change your life.

We spent the week in Colorado serving alongside other missionaries. The WMU® had prayed over the participants. Placing us in groups around the city. We were assigned to a church planter from Texas at Living Hope Fellowship. Paired with groups from Louisiana, Arkansas, Texas, and Illinois.

Our week consisted of spending time with local kids at the park, back yard Bible clubs, and light construction work. We loved every minute of it. Realizing on this trip that this is what we were made for. These people were like family even though we had only known them a few days. I remember the kids saying that they had never made friends so fast before. "That's because these people aren't just random strangers. They are our church family," I replied. We were brothers and sisters in Christ.

We left Colorado knowing we had found our calling. But not very sure of what good we had done. Yes we had played with the kids, helped with crafts, and fixed fences. We had prayed with people and invited them to the local church.

That's what we did at home, nothing special, just churchy stuff. From the missionary videos we had seen in church it seemed other people made a lot bigger impact than we felt we had.

After arriving back home we were supposed to report to the church what we had accomplished. We knew all the physical things we had done. Although we were struggling to see the spiritual fruit. What had come of it? What impact had we made?

All these people had rallied behind us and supported us. For what, to do crafts with kids? How could I stand in front of the church and express to them what we had accomplished? When we weren't even sure ourselves.

At this point a few weeks had went by. We were definitely putting off reporting to the church about the mission trip. Still struggling through how we would handle every ones reaction to the fact we had only managed to do normal churchy stuff on our first mission trip.

Unexpectedly we received a letter in the mail. It was from the pastor in Colorado expressing how much of an impact our group had had on the community. The children and families had noticed how we interacted with each other and with them. I guess doing regular churchy stuff did stand out to the community. I had forgotten how different church people behaved compared to people outside the church.

Church people had stood out to me at the beginning too. How generous they were through the free meals and activities. How kind they were to come to our house each week for Bible studies.

How welcoming they were through the home school group. That's what had attracted me to them. That's what had pushed me to want to give Jesus a chance.

That's exactly what had impacted the kids and families in that community. Had it really taken only three years of being a church person for me to take for granted the impact my behavior can have on a hurting world. I realized my behavior may not stand out inside that church surrounded by only Christians but it surely will outside those doors. Most of all It will standout when a lost person walks in those doors.

These families were making the same decision to allow God to have their lives as Bubba and I had. God had used all the things we thought were normal churchy activities to eternally change the lives of those families. We were hooked! We had the privilege to be a part of the greatest job in the world. To be used by God to help save His people.

1 John 4:19 We love because he first loved us.

Chapter 6

The WMU® holds this type of mission trip once a year. It's called Family Fest®. Designed for families with children over age 6. This next one would be held in Kentucky. We had plans to work with some of the same families we had worked with on the Colorado trip.

Preparing for this mission trip was by far less stressful. We knew how to fundraise. Speaking in front of the church wasn't that bad anymore. We thought we knew what to expect. We had seen what God had done in Colorado. We were determined to be used in mighty ways on this trip also. This is what we were made for. We had also experienced how much Satan (the enemy) does not like missions.

God was in control. We would not allow the enemy to steal our joy or mess up what God had planned for us to do. Learning to pray with purpose and rebuking Satan are valuable tools. Learned quickly when necessary.

When the dryer broke about a month before the trip. We were determined to stay positive. We've waited all year for this mission trip. This was not going to get us down. I loved hanging clothes on the line anyway. "Ha, nice try Satan!" We just kept praising Jesus and rebuking the enemy's schemes.

About a week later as I went to get my clothes out of the washer I found myself standing in a puddle of water. The washer tub had cracked. Repairing it was not an option. We would need a new one. All I could do was laugh. "Really, Satan?"

We had spent quite a bit of time intrigued by homesteading. Hand washing clothes had always been something that interested me. I can't say I ever wanted it to be my only way of washing clothes, especially with a trip coming up. Getting the equipment to hand wash would be far less expensive than a new washer and dryer. Which is also, I believe, the only reason Bubba agreed to it.

We purchased the wringer, some five-gallon buckets, and a portable washer (resembles a plunger with holes). Bubba then built me a little station in the yard. I had everything I needed to wash our clothes. The next day I would head out first thing in the morning to do laundry.

It didn't take me long to realize that I loved hand washing clothes. The simplicity, the peace, and quiet. This took so much time that I had to be intentional about how I spent my time. I would wash, wring, and hang for hours while listening to Christian music. The kids were involved in the process a lot. Sometimes just sitting out there for hours with me.

I hadn't realized how busy I'd gotten just doing church stuff. I wasn't actually living in communion with God anymore but rather just working for Him. It was clear the change had taken place a while ago. I hadn't felt this much peace in a long time. This time with God was amazing. I couldn't wait to go out and wash clothes every day.

A few people literally thought I was crazy. They may have thought I was lying about enjoying it. That I was just making the best out of a bad situation. Which is how the idea had first come about. Now it was something totally different. Now it was something I needed. Something I thought about all day. Something I longed for.

The Kentucky trip was every bit as great as the Colorado. We met even more amazing, like minded people. These trips are designed to help the local churches reach the people around them better. The pastor we were assigned to had been an international missionary. He had recently moved back to the states to serve in this community. On the first Sunday we met at his church, Thompsonville Baptist Church, to attend service with the regulars.

As I sat in that service God spoke to my heart so clearly. "Kitty Hawk doesn't own you; I do." The pastor had said nothing of the sort. Yet, the message was so clear to me. I immediately knew what it meant. We had been waiting for our home church, Kitty Hawk Baptist, to release us. To tell us it was time to leave the beach. Just like the mission trip. We had sat waiting for Kitty Hawk to send us when it was clear God was telling us to go.

I'm going to pause in our journey here to explain something. When I say God spoke to my heart those words and I immediately knew what they meant. That is exactly what I mean. It wasn't a random thought that popped into my head. It wasn't a feeling I decided to run with. The only way I can explain it is in my heart I heard those words. A few years back if someone would have told me this I would have thought they were crazy. So I guess it's something you understand when it happens. I wish He spoke to me often like that but He doesn't. I also want to point out that we had known for almost three years at this point that He would move us from the beach. We had many confirmations throughout the years pertaining to us leaving. Others were even able to discern that God would call us away. Maybe He had to be so blunt in that church in Kentucky because we weren't picking up on the confirmations. I know for a fact we had willing hearts the whole time. We just weren't getting the hint. It's encouraging to know our lack of experience can't even stop God from accomplishing His goals in our lives.

Back to the story. My head was spinning with plans, timelines, and details. We had so much to process and pray about. I wished I were back home with my wringer to think and spend time in prayer. Although right now we really needed to focus on the mission He had us on. I needed to calm my thoughts down. I needed to wait on His direction. These people deserved our full attention. The ones He had sent us here to minister to.

On this mission trip we participated in similar community outreaches as we had on the first trip. Light construction work, visiting with people, and spending time with families at the park. We didn't need to see the impact we had in order to know that we had made an impact. Some people plant the seeds of faith while others see the harvest. We were finally ok with that.

One family we met at the park home schooled. She also hand washed clothes for a season and loved it. I wasn't crazy! It's amazing when God sends people into our lives at just the right time to encourage us. Specially, when we think we are the ones supposed to encourage them.

On this mission trip I also realized sometimes God gives us experience in an area that may seem pointless at the time. At the park I spotted a group I could assist. The group was responsible for handing out tons of hotdogs. They needed to come off the grill, be placed in buns, and wrapped in foil. I knew I could help with this.

Thinking back to our beach hotdog handouts where we had spent hours on Saturdays. Wrapping and handing out hotdogs to over a hundred visitors with our church. As I started helping I felt like a professional hotdog wrapper. I was receiving a few funny looks. People were probably wondering why I was so good at this. I couldn't help but laugh at how many hotdogs I had wrapped and handed to people to prepare me for that moment. During those hotdog handouts it never crossed my mind that He was preparing me for something in the future. I have started to think differently about experiences that I once thought were irrelevant or at the least not church related.

One evening after a very long day of serving in Kentucky we received a call from Bubba's parents wanting to get into our house. The church had contacted them and wanted to gift us with a washer and dryer.

My worst nightmare was literally happening right now! Right in the middle of my perfect mission trip. This may sound silly and completely ungrateful to you. So, let me explain part of why this was such a huge problem for me.

When the washing machine broke it flooded the laundry room which resulted in the wet walls and part of the floor being torn out. The washer was on the side porch and you could literally see under the master bathtub from the kitchen. We were packing and rushing to leave so the house was not in "in-law" condition. To make matters worse, the evening before the trip our kitchen sink busted and started spraying all over the kitchen. We turned it off, cleaned it up, and taped it off. Yes, we taped it off. "Satan, you are not winning!" If you can picture what my house looked like. Than you can see why I didn't want my in-laws in the house nor anyone from the church.

The worst part, I did not want that washer and dryer. I needed to hand wash. Especially after the message we had just received in that service. I needed that time with God in the backyard more than ever.

Obviously, I still had the ability to pray and spend time with God with a washer and dryer. But I knew myself. I knew my weaknesses and my flaws. I knew I would go right back to being too busy. This was extremely important. I needed to do whatever I could to make sure I would spend that time in prayer. For me that meant spending hours hand washing, playing Christian music, praying, and listening to God.

I frantically called my mentor at church begging her to make it stop. I know I sounded incredibly ungrateful. Thankfully she understood. She called it off. As I got off the phone I realized what I had just done. I had just called off a church wide blessing for us. I can only imagine the pastor's face when she told him we were refusing something the church had worked together to bless us with.

Psalm 46:10 He says, "Be still, and know that I am God: I will be exalted among the nations, I will be exalted in the earth."

Chapter 7

Countless hours were spent in that backyard praying and asking God the same questions repeatedly. "Are you really telling us it's time to go? Are you sure? Am I just crazy?" I can laugh about it now because every time I asked, I already knew the answer. Each day I would head back outside to do it all over again. Each day recognizing that small voice that I had heard so much about. Never quite understanding it, until now.

I believe I kept seeking reassurance because we were scared. Not scared of following but scared we would mess this up. Bubba would be quitting his job at the cabinet shop. Which he's had for the past fourteen years. We were going to sell our home and had no idea where we were going. From an earthly perspective this looked crazy. We looked crazy. Regardless of how it looked it felt completely ok. This must be what peace that surpasses all understanding feels like.

Each day outside was spent pleading with God. "If this is not your will, stop us! Don't let us ruin our lives." Each day I had the same assurance. It was like God was just humoring me. Patiently answering the same questions hundreds of times.

We asked everyone we knew to pray with us. To help us seek God's direction. To be completely honest, I think some were praying because they thought we were confused and making a big mistake.

We sought God's Word and I immersed myself in Bible studies trying to find anything that could help us. Secretly trying to speed

Him up giving us direction. Learning along the way He doesn't work that way.

The verse I lived by became, Philippians 4:9. Trying to think back to anything we had been taught or had seen. One thing that really helped me was remembering that God directs Bubba and I towards the same things.

Here's an example. Before the first mission trip to Colorado, literally weeks before. While working in the garden I suddenly felt we should take his twin niece and nephew with us. All hotels were previously booked and deadline for registration had ended. Honestly tacking on two more teens for a fifty four hour round trip car ride did not sound smart to me. This didn't make any sense at all while feeling ok. Therefore, this must be God's idea.

"God, if this is what you want us to do, tell Bubba." I was determined to not say anything to him about it. Two hours later he texts from work. "Do you think we should take the twins?" I reply, "Yes!" Then I start thinking, "What if it's too late?" His reply, "I already emailed the director it's not too late." And that's how our God works.

Back to the situation at hand and putting into practice what we had learned or been taught. We knew He would lead us both in the same direction.

It was very hard trying to tell family and friends that we were selling our home and moving without knowing where we were going. It's hard to look at people you love and say you're leaving simply because Jesus told you to. Even if they are Christians you still sound crazy. The fact that we were "new" Christians didn't make it any easier. I'm sure they were terrified for us. Maybe even a little skeptical of whether we had heard God at all.

We really needed to be confident in what we were doing. We are followers of Jesus. He had told us to pack up and leave. He had not told us where yet and that was ok. Those were the hardest words to say out loud. Even if in my back yard I knew they were true.

We learned the enemy's schemes were not limited to appliance murder. He'd been going around for years messing with our confidence. We hadn't even known it. I'm thankful that although we were not confident in our own abilities we were confident in God's ability. We didn't need to have it all figured out. We just needed to cling to the one that did. We would need God's power in us to accomplish this. We would need his power to defend why we were doing this to people who had been Christians longer than we'd been alive. We learned there is a calling on our lives. We will stand firm in who we are in Christ. We will stand firm in who Christ says we are and what He has called us to do.

Before listing it with a realtor God would lay it on my heart to approach a friend of ours about buying our house. They needed time to pray before making a decision to buy.

God spoke to them rather quickly that buying our house was the right decision for them. As we started the process, we realized we were selling our house before knowing where we were going.

Philippians 4:9 Whatever you have learned or received or heard from me, or seen in me-put it into practice. And the God of peace will be with you.

Chapter 8

W e tried to focus on the things we knew He was telling us
rather than all the details we didn't know yet. We knew
our new home would be in the U.S. Praying and searching the map
we really felt like Tennessee was it or somewhere in that area. We
started looking for property and jobs. If that's where God wanted
us then that's where we'd go.

A trip had been planned to visit the family we'd met from
Louisiana on the mission trip. We decided to take a route through
Tennessee. Giving us a great opportunity to seek guidance from
God about which area in Tennessee He was calling us to. Seemed
to all be falling right into place.

Again, we reached out to our church family and friends for
prayer. Asking them to pray specifically for closed doors to areas we
were not supposed to go. Having people in your life that you can
call on for prayer is so important. We were intentional about our
prayers. Constantly trying our best to discern what God wanted
from us. Praying about which direction He wanted us to go.

The further we got into Tennessee the more we both knew He
wasn't sending us there. The prayers had worked. Not in the way
we had expected or hoped, but they had worked. We were sure He
was not sending us to Tennessee.

Maybe it's just me but I was hoping we would drive past a for
sale sign while God hollered through the clouds, "Welcome home!"
Why can't life be that simple? Instead we received that small voice
saying, "No, this isn't it."

In that moment this great fun adventure had taken a turn for the worst. We had started this trip to Louisiana praying God would close doors and direct us. All while assuming we were right about Tennessee. Assuming we had already figured it all out, that our testimony would be so great. *Family is directed by God to move from the beach. They already have a trip planned to see friends from a mission trip. They drive through prospected state. Find their new home. Come back, sell house, and move. Praising God the whole way.*

Doesn't sound wrong! It actually sounds a lot like what everyone had said to us, "Things with God just fall right into place." We realized our story didn't look like that. Our story looked like we had buyers for our house and we were moving to nowhere. Great!

Out of desperation I grab my Bible study books and open to the page I was on. Though not the page the rest of the class was on. I always manage to be a few days or lessons behind the rest of the class. But God always seems to meet me right where I'm at. I'm not sure what I was expecting although I was surely not expecting what I got.

I look down at the page in front of me and begin to read a passage about God telling Abraham to go. God had not yet told him where he was going. Abraham obeyed without knowing. Abraham literally packed his stuff up and started walking before he knew where he was going.

I didn't know which tears to cry. Tears because the God of the universe knows exactly where I'm at and He meets me there. He knew exactly when I would open that book. Literally the exact hour we left Tennessee. Or tears because the confirmation I just asked for and received from God said flat out that we could be moving before knowing where we were going.

I took a photo of the page. Sending it to practically everyone I knew. We needed more prayer than I thought. As I sat in shock, I began to receive replies about the photo. Messages similar to these. "That's so cool! Wow, that's crazy! No way!" All I could think was, "Wow! No way! You know what's crazy, us! We are driving down the interstate with our kids in the backseat practically playing Eenie Meenie Miny Mo with the states in America!"

This was around the time I decided I could reason with God and get Him to see my point of view. Our conversations went something like this. "God, we cannot just sell our house, quit our job, pack up our kids, and leave in a truck going nowhere. Can't we get arrested for stuff like this? This does not sound like faith. It sounds irresponsible."

Our thoughts began to change after praying and just being in His presence. Funny how taking your eyes off your problems and directing them back to your savior can change your perspective. We would do it! We knew we would do whatever He asked of us. God had proven to us that He could be trusted.

Bubba turned to me and said, "If we have to pack the truck and drive until He tells us where, than we will." I wasn't sure if I should be proud of my husband's faith or afraid of it.

During the remainder of the trip I worked through my dialogue with God. That small voice telling me, "It's all going to be ok." Bubba seemed sure God would confirm to us where we were going. I just needed to try and have that same level of faith. I wanted so badly to just know what was going on. To know the plan. To have some sort of control over this.

It didn't take long before we got some of the confirmation we needed. As we crossed the Mississippi River Bubba looked at me and said, "It's on this side." I could tell he was as sure as I had been in that church in Kentucky. Yes! Almost half the country was eliminated from our search. It seemed God was giving us just enough direction to keep us moving toward what He wanted.

Obviously, the only thing on our minds when we arrived at our friend's house was finding out which area He was directing us to. So, we started looking around their area specifically east Texas. Thinking maybe meeting this couple on the mission trip was part of the plan. Since there are no coincidences with God, it surely is not random chance we are here currently on this journey. It's on the correct side of the Mississippi after all and we were open to anywhere. East Texas seemed like as good of a place as any.

While on this trip we continued praying for direction. We trusted God would close doors as needed. We both felt we liked this area. We felt hope as we left to head home. Telling God we would pursue east Texas until He stopped us.

Hebrews 11:8 By faith Abraham, when called to go to a place he would later receive as his inheritance, obeyed and went, even though he did not know where he was going.

Chapter 9

Ａfter heading out to wash clothes I realized I had no desire to do this. I started thinking to myself, "This is insane. Who would do this for hours every day?" I had been hand washing clothes for five months now. Feeling like I couldn't live without it. I'd spent hours praying and seeking guidance on the biggest decision of our lives while washing. I had loved it. Everything in me had needed this. Needed it like I needed food to survive. What had changed?

As I sat praying, I realized the desire had gone away right after we started looking into east Texas. Could it mean we had found our answer? It had to mean that. Nothing else could explain it.

I had developed a prayer habit. A quiet time with God, which surrounded this wringer. I had no desire to hand wash these clothes though I had loved the time spent doing it. The deep desire to need something. To need the time with God so badly that I had given up scheduling things in our lives because it took from my time with Him.

Now, what should I do? I don't want to hand wash these clothes anymore. Though I still have a family with dirty clothes. A lot of them since we just got back from a trip. Could I really suck up my pride enough to call my mentor and tell her I wanted the washer and dryer after all? Can you even do that, refuse a blessing than ask for it later?

That wasn't even the biggest problem. Some people thought I was crazy for doing this in the first place. That it was just a phase I would get over. Wouldn't it look like they were right? But it wasn't a phase, it was God. He had used this time to allow me to focus. I grew so much in that time. I learned to trust Him even when my understanding was telling me something different. I learned that He will direct our paths. I learned we didn't need to see the whole staircase to know it was ok to take another step. I can recognize that small voice now. To recognize that when He's trying to "still" me it's because something big is coming up and I don't want to miss it. How could I just let everyone think this had been just a wanna-be homesteading phase that I had gotten over?

Little did I know I was learning the hardest lesson yet. People will think you're crazy when you radically follow God. People may think you're irresponsible and reckless. You may lose family and friends because they cannot see what you see. That's ok. People thought Jesus was crazy. Jesus lost friends because they didn't see what He saw. Why would we be any different?

I needed to realize that it didn't matter what people thought. I went to Bubba trying to convince him to call the pastor and ask if we could still get the machines. He rarely bails me out of situations that I should handle myself. Therefore, he did not think this was a great idea. To be honest I was the one who had acted so irrationally in Kentucky. Calling off the whole washing machine blessing in the first place. I needed to handle this myself. I called my mentor and tried to explain. Praise Jesus she had never actually called it off. She only had it put on hold. Not everyone would understand why I had the desire in the first place or why it had all changed. That's ok. God knew and that's all that mattered.

Romans 8:31 What, then, shall we say in response to these things? If God is for us, who can be against us?

Chapter 10

By the time Bubba received a job offer with a land surveying company we were already looking into properties, houses, and realtors in east Texas. The company was owned by the family we had met on the mission trip. He had no experience in that area of work other than navigating maps while scoping out hunting properties, but that's ok. We were confident God could handle the details. Bubba would go to school to get a degree, if needed. Things were looking up. We had an area. He had a job. Selling the house was going great. Family and friends were starting to understand we were really leaving. Bubba had already put in his notice for work. Giving plenty of time to help train the person replacing him. This was real. And it was happening real quick. Things were falling "right into place" finally. Just like everyone had said.

A few weeks later everything changed. Nadia reinjured herself at the park. She had sustained an injury to her knee when she was younger. Since that time her kneecap would slip out of place. Although extremely painful, we could usually just pop it back into place. Surgery to solve the problem had not been an option. The doctors had told us we needed to wait until her bones had finished growing.

We realized quickly this time was different and took her to the emergency room. They informed us she had torn the ligament that held her kneecap on. There would be no popping this one back in. We were referred to a specialist. At the specialist we were told she had grown enough to have the surgery if physical therapy couldn't remedy the issue. Giving us a month to see if physical therapy would be enough. All the places near us were full. We ended up having to go over an hour away to physical therapy.

This was not my plan! How could things have changed so drastically? So much for everything falling into place. I did not have time for this! I was barely holding it all together as is. All of this never changed the fact that we were still selling our house. Packing and moving across the country in six months with nowhere to go. We were pretty sure on which state. Though we were not sure which town or house. To make matters worse Nadia and I had already been through this physical therapy thing. It was a nightmare. It's hard enough to parent a teen at times. Let alone be their teacher and now physical therapist.

As I sat in Mom's Group asking for prayer. Pretty much venting about my circumstances. One of the moms helped me see a different perspective. Yes, these were all facts. They were really happening but they weren't truth. They weren't God's truth. She spoke life over our circumstances. Praying this time driving would be quality time with God. Praying this would bring Nadia and I closer than we've ever been. Her prayer would change my perspective on many things to come. The facts may say one thing. What does God's truth say?

Our one month deadline came and went. We were not going to avoid surgery. Really avoiding it wasn't best for her. The surgery wasn't a sure thing but it was the best chance she had. In the meantime the physical therapy was to prepare her for surgery. We needed to reduce the swelling enough to operate.

We had physical therapy sometimes three times a week. Still at the children's hospital, over an hour away. Having it so far away meant it would take us almost six hours from the time we left the house to the time we got back home. Short distances she could use crutches. Anything further she needed a wheelchair.

We saw God's provision in everything. Even in the washing machine flooding those walls. Bubba had taken that opportunity to redo our bathroom. Which was directly behind the washer. He had put in a large walk in stone shower. Which now fit her shower chair perfectly. What the enemy had meant for evil, God had used for good.

She and I began to look forward to those rides to physical therapy. We were becoming closer just as had been prayed over us. I was beginning to need that time driving to pray and seek God.

The facts said we had a lot to be upset about. The truth said we had a lot to praise God for. We continued to press into Him the best we knew how and He continued to come through for us.

Psalm 46:1 God is our refuge and strength,
an ever-present help in trouble.

Chapter 11

We were determined to be in the exact area God wanted us in. That's a lot of pressure. We would need all the prayers we could get. Our church family, Bible study ladies, and Mom's Group were right there by our side praying with us.

We were beginning to realize just how large of an area east Texas really was. We had selected a realtor. Feeling like he was the right one for this journey we were on. We continued searching the online resources the best we could from afar. On more than one occasion the houses we had interest in were every bit of an hour away from him. He always seemed willing to travel for us.

He saw firsthand God's way of leading us. Pretty much by process of elimination. We would contact him about each house we had an interest in. Only to be told by the end of the day that they were no longer available. Either because they were sold or under contract. Quite a few going under contract the very day we showed interest. These were doors closing for sure.

House after house getting our hopes up only to be let down. We knew we had prayed for doors to close but this was a little overboard. We began to just expect the let down every time he called or text. God had made it very clear that He was running this show. We continued picking out houses all over east Texas and we continued losing houses.

It became kind of a joke between us and the realtor that we were helping the real estate business in each area we showed interest in. It was funny. At the same time getting on my nerves. We were getting all the closed doors we needed to direct us. I wanted some open ones.

We needed to be brave to face the doubts. It was hard. People started to think He was closing the door all together. I understood why they thought that. How could we stand in front of them and say He was still calling us to east Texas? When it was so clear He was closing way more doors in the area than He was opening.

We could because we still had the confirmations. The ones He had already given us. We had asked for Him to close doors. To not allow us to go in the wrong direction. He was answering our specific prayer. We began to hear things similar to, "Maybe God had just tested you to see if you would obey. Maybe He really didn't want you to go but rather just be willing to go."

Praise the Lord, I knew that one wasn't true. The year before He had tested me. Laying it on my heart to reach out to the area I had grown up in, rural New York. I obeyed. Reaching out to churches and old friends. Sharing events the local churches were having. Praying for the people and churches. I was beginning to sense He was telling us to move there. My response was a quick, "Oh no, Lord! Not happening!"

I'll never forget the dialogue that took place between God and I during those days. I was fighting with every ounce of me. I had good reason to fight. I was into every bad thing I could get my hands on in that town when I was a teen. Blaming it on the place at the time. I had thanked God numerous times for bringing me out of there and moving me to North Carolina. How could He send me back? Especially, now that I had my own kids to worry about.

I felt so much shame and guilt while telling God no. I knew exactly what He was asking of me and I was refusing. Sunday comes and I'm standing during worship at church. I realize I can't worship my God at the same time as disobeying a direct order. As tears roll down my face I humbly say, "God, I'll go where you send me."

Just as quickly as the words left my mouth, I knew He wasn't sending me. After the service, I frantically went to the pastor's wife to ask her, "What had just happened?" She helped me to understand God was testing my obedience. There had been one place in the entire world I would not go for Him. Until that day when my faith became bigger than my fear.

After that experience I could confidently say, He was not "testing" us with east Texas. He was sending us for real. We didn't know why and at this point in our walk that was irrelevant. God had proven to be worth listening to and following.

We would need to stand on what we knew. What He had already confirmed. I remember feeling like I was being held up by the fact that our friends were Christians and they had prayed to buy our house. Unless His plan had been for us to live together like one big happy family than He must have meant for us to move.

It's ok to be held up by someone else's faith for a short time. Part of why we are all the body of Christ. It was also ok that we sometimes doubted our own ability to be led. However, it was not ok to ever doubt God's ability to lead us. He would come through. He always had. He always would.

We worked out a plan with our friends. Since we would be closing on our house before we could leave the beach. We would pay them rent and stay in our home. This way we wouldn't have to move twice within a few months.

Of course, we realized some mortgages do not allow you to do that. This being one of those mortgages. Obviously, these had just been our plans and not God's plan. The new buyers would need to be moved in within a certain number of days after closing.

Our friends had decided to keep their previous home. The new plan would be to swap houses with them until it was time for us to leave. God's provision was still there. It just didn't look like we had expected. It didn't look anything like my plan had.

Our lives were still consumed with our weekly trips to physical therapy. Sometimes up to three times a week. Swelling had gone down on her knee and surgery was scheduled for April 19th. The moving day had already been decided for April 14th. The thought of surgery four days after moving was terrifying. To make matters worse we were still looking for a place in east Texas.

Our facts looked pretty bad at this point. Though His truth remained the same. God doesn't change. No matter how our circumstances looked. His promises will be true forever. He has called us to this. Therefore, He will see us through it. We would need to keep our focus on Him the best we knew how.

Romans 4:20 Yet he did not waver through unbelief regarding the promise of God, but was strengthened in his faith and gave glory to God,

Chapter 12

Time was running out for us to make another trip to Texas. We found a few houses online. Surprisingly they were still on the market. The only time we were able to go fell seventeen days before the house switch with surgery four days after.

We knew a lot of doors had been closing in east Texas. We also knew there had been enough confirmations to keep us heading in that direction. We were being obedient through many trials to what He had called. Surely, He would bless us on this trip. We weren't asking for much, just a home.

Our plan was to go look at the houses we had found online. Call the realtor to meet us at the ones we wanted to pursue. In our minds we had already decided by a long shot on one house. So naturally we went there first. Both of us excited and expectant. I was relieved. At last, the search would be over. Finally, we would have the answers and the uncertainty would be behind us.

As we pulled into the driveway of the first house we knew right away this house was not our house. It was obvious to both of us. I got out of the car and began to walk around the house. Hoping God would change His mind. Looking off into the field behind the house. Trying hard to change the fact that He was clearly telling us this wasn't it. Squeezing my eyes shut like a little kid wishing that when I opened my eyes everything would be different. That if I prayed hard enough the answer I had received would change.

I had wanted this to be it so bad. I had so many expectations before arriving. Expectations that this would all work out my way.

I didn't want to have faith anymore. Hadn't we "walked by faith" enough? All I wanted was answers. What had we done so wrong to deserve this? This didn't feel at all like a blessing. This felt like a punishment. I had put all my hope in this house. Not so much the house but the hope of knowing which house.

We continued our search. Heading to the other houses we had picked out before arriving. Feeling defeated but unwilling to give up. As we pulled up to each house, we knew right away each house was not the one. At this point I'm not sure I even would have heard God. My heart wasn't in it anymore.

We weren't being picky. None of them were big or fancy houses. They were all in our price range. They all needed work. We only had a few days to figure this out.

We scrambled and reached for any leads. Driving around for hours in all directions from our hotel. Each time we found a house we'd call the realtor to see if it was still available. Either to be told by him it wasn't or by God that it wasn't ours.

I honestly don't remember how many houses we tried to get on this trip. I'm ashamed to admit towards the end of this week I didn't even care what God wanted. Hadn't we done enough? Hadn't we been obedient enough? I started to mold and spin scriptures to fit my will. Hadn't He called us to care for and provide for our kids? Well guess what? That meant a house.

This is when we went and looked at the big fancy one. With way more bells and whistles than we needed or wanted. Didn't require any work and wasn't under the amount we had agreed to stay under.

I made it so obvious I wanted that house that Bubba was willing to go along with me. After all we had no other options. This was the last day before heading back to the beach.

We called the realtor. Making it clear that this house was the one. I knew God wasn't behind this house and I didn't care. I sent the link to everyone I knew. Asking them to pray that "Satan" did not mess this up for me. "I am getting a house before we leave this place," I thought. No matter what it takes.

The responses I received were in love but hilarious. My friends were trying to express to me that it was indeed a beautiful house. But it didn't seem right for many reasons. To have friends that are not just there to tell you what you want to hear is very important. I heard them. Although, I didn't listen to them at the time.

On our way back to the beach we received a call from the realtor. He was calling to inform us the owner was no longer willing to sell. "Oh, really! You just have your house for sale because you don't want to sell it," I thought. I was furious with God! He had went behind my back and convinced that man to change his mind. I was completely irrational at this point.

Our control over our circumstances had been taken, again. It was clear that God was in control. I had tried my best to take the reins. I had tried to rally all my little Christian friends to support my will. I had rebuked "Satan" not to mess up my plans. I had cried, pleaded, and begged. And guess what? God was still in control.

One thing I had control over was how I responded to my circumstances. Would I handle this gracefully or like a blubbering idiot? The facts were scary. I needed to find God's truth in this.

How quickly I had forgotten what God had said when I had taken my eyes off of Him. At this point I wasn't believing He was behind us. Maybe others were right. Maybe we were just irresponsible new Christians thinking we heard God.

I messaged a friend from Mom's Group. Out of desperation I explained all that had happened. She replied, "Just because plans do not turn out the way we expect or hope. Does not mean God is not behind us."

Searching my Bible study books for answers. I came across a passage talking about praying to have eyes to see and ears to hear. I was at one of the most desperate times I can remember passing through Alabama. Hiding my face so the kids couldn't see my tears. I look out the window and pray, "Lord, give me eyes to see and ears to hear what you're telling us to do." Just then the bridge over-pass flashes, "Have courage." A small beat up car zooms next to us. Cuts in front of us and weaves off into traffic. The car is sporting Texas license plates.

Wasn't it ironic the message came through an impatient, worn out, and barely holding it together car? That's exactly how I felt; impatient, worn out, and barely holding it together. Ok God. It's Texas. I'll continue to be brave. This little gesture from God was powerful and sustaining. Yet, practically impossible to explain to others. It was exactly what I needed to keep me from giving up.

This whole trip I had been directing myself and saying it was God. Yes, God called us to move. Yes, God was calling us to this area. But I was in no way talking to Him and being led step by step by Him. I had taken His initial direction and ran with it.

I needed scriptures to keep me focused. Logically I looked online, "Scriptures for buying a house." I was able to find many scriptures online that were helpful. Matthew 6:33 But seek first his kingdom and his righteousness, and all these things will be given to you as well. Psalm 37:4 Take delight in the LORD, and he will give you the desires of your heart. Deuteronomy 11:31 take possession of the land the Lord your God is giving you. Joshua 24:13 I have given you a land for which you did not labor NKJV. Were these scriptures saying God would be the one to do it? That He would work it all out?

I didn't quite understand that but I knew enough to realize we were striving. We were trying to do it ourselves. I was terrified to face all the questions when we arrived back home. If it was hard for us to understand what God was calling us to do considering we were living it. I could only imagine how hard it was for others to understand.

We would be faced with the doubts. Having to explain why we were still doing this. These people loved our family. They wanted what was best for us. We knew this was the reason they were scared. We were scared too.

2 Timothy 2:13 If we are faithless, he remains faithful, for he cannot disown himself.

Chapter 13

We arrived home and started packing. We were moving to Texas! The fact that we had no idea what house or town was irrelevant. God had confirmed to us it was Texas.

It was difficult deciding what to take with so many questions still unanswered. Would we have a yard for our garden stuff? Would we be able to have chickens? Should we bring the chicken stuff just in case? Would we have a garage or shed for tools? What furniture should we bring?

We ended up selling or giving away most of our belongings. Deciding that would be better than paying to move it. Possibly having to get rid of it if we ended up not having enough space. Also the house we were switching into, while waiting to move, was smaller. Nadia would be navigating it with a wheelchair or crutches anyway. She would need as much space as possible. Whatever we decided to keep would stay packed for the next three months until leaving the beach.

For me the hardest part was leaving our house. I had lived in this house longer than I've lived anywhere in my life. It was way more than just a house. It was our home. We had built a life here. I also despised change. Change meant instability. Lately not much of anything felt stable in our lives.

I'd walk around that yard crying as I thought about our memories. The Gardenia's Nadia had picked for her teachers at the end of the school years. When she was in public school. Reminiscing over all the flowers that came up every year. Praying over the strawberry patch I worked so hard to start. Biggest crop of three strawberries. The chicken coop that had once been a dog kennel. Crying as I thought of Limpy the injured Guinea hen David had fostered for a year. The plans we had for this house and yard. Picturing the buckets of Muscadine grapes we had picked over the years. Turning them into jellies and sauces. Thinking about the many walks down our street. From the days of babies in strollers to my youngest being almost as tall as me. Many of our neighbors knew us. Some were even family. Always having the opportunity to stop and chat. Waving at everyone as they drove by.

I felt like someone else would be living my life. I had expected this to be easy. "Things with God were easy and just fall into place." At least that's what everyone had said. This was not easy. This was the hardest thing I had ever done. This house was my stability. This life I had created was my stability. Soon it would all be gone.

Maybe I wasn't brave. Maybe I wanted to call it all off and stay right here. Y'all, the struggle was real. I was terrified. As I sat sobbing, "Lord, why are you doing this?" I was reminded by that small voice. The voice I had come to recognize, "Fear doesn't decide if you follow." Fear was directing me to back away and stay here. Faith was directing me to follow God wherever He may lead. Our facts were scary but His truth remained the same.

He had called us to this. He would see us through it. That was the truth. My facts were irrelevant when lined up against God's truth. The fact that I was sick with fear daily never once changed God's truth. He remained the same. The confirmations He had shown us were still true even if my feelings had changed. God did not and will not change His mind regardless of how many times I may change mine. That's stability! That's the stability I should find comfort in.

The day we would switch houses was approaching. I was so upset about our plans not working, surgery coming up, and leaving our home. I was not able to see God's provision by us switching houses with our friends. How much harder this would have been had we needed to find somewhere to rent at the beach in the middle of vacation season.

The day came and we switched houses. It all went about as smoothly as it could have. Kind of felt like packing and preparing for a huge camping trip. Only to unpack everything that same day when you get to your campsite. One thing on your mind. To get everything set up enough for the kids to sleep.

The next four days were spent preparing the house and Nadia's room for post-surgery. The day of her surgery arrived, and it went great. Only physical therapy would determine if she would recover fully. My life had been so turned upside down and our control taken so many times that I didn't even feel like I could try and lead. I was relying as much as possible on God and His leading. I did not want to get off the path He had for us. I knew physically and emotionally I couldn't handle straying off the path again.

Proverbs 3:5-6 Trust in the LORD with all your heart and lean not on your own understanding; In all your ways acknowledge Him and He shall direct your paths. NKJV

Chapter 14

About a week later the realtor called. He had come across a house that he thought fit our criteria. Surely this is what the scriptures meant. Scriptures about not laboring for it. We didn't look for it. He called us, right?

Bubba and his brother immediately made plans to fly out to look at it. Neither had been on a plane before. But this was important. He needed to step foot in the house before agreeing to buy it. He also decided he wanted to have three houses to look at. We looked on the real estate sites. Picking two more houses that were still on the market.

I needed to stay behind to take care of Nadia after surgery. I really wanted to be on that plane heading to our new home. It was unfair he would be able to see it and I would have to wait until we moved. Although this would make it easier for God to lead him without my feelings getting in the way.

They arrived in Texas. Determined and hopeful to pick a house. Maybe God didn't care which house. Maybe He just wanted us to be obedient in going. We decided we were going to just pick one. No matter what happened this weekend he would choose a house that would become our home.

Within hours of being in Texas they had eliminated one of the houses. It was out of our price range. It just so happened to be the one the realtor had called us about.

We continued in "our" plan. Praying God would reveal to us which one of the houses left was our home. We were determined to have a house picked out before they returned. Funny how fast we went back to our own plan all while asking God to bless it.

Bubba felt like this was his responsibility. To provide a home for his family. If I felt like people were staring at me like a wacko for everything we were doing, imagine how he felt. He was the head of our house. He provided for us. To others it looked very irresponsible to pack your family up, quit your good job, and move them with nowhere to go. He was going to do his job and provide us a house.

As Bubba walked through the first house. He knew it wasn't the one. I had already ignored every red flag about this house. Convincing Bubba to give it another shot. Convincing myself I could make it work. To the point I could picture us living there, enjoying the features.

I have a wonderful imagination. Allowing me to build up a whole scenario in my head to be upset about when it doesn't work out. A whole life missed out on and it never even happened. The sunroom my plants already loved. My clothesline I enjoyed hanging clothes on. Maybe I was just losing my mind.

At this point in my imagination my family had lived in every house we showed interest in. In the short number of hours it had taken for the realtor to inform us the houses weren't on the market I had already made a life there. Just to have it all taken away. Yep, I was losing my mind for sure.

There was no amount of convincing that I could do. He and I both knew this house was not our home.

Bubba went with the realtor to the last house. He walked through. It was nice. The neighborhood was nice. We liked it. Honestly, we had no other choice. We were leaving the beach in two months. He put in an offer. Offering asking price since we didn't have time to be messing around negotiating prices. We finally had a house. Flying back the next day they had accomplished their goal of choosing our house.

The next day the realtor calls. He's unhappy to tell us the news. Someone had come the same day and offered more. Of course, the seller accepted. I was devastated! I felt so mad at God. How could this happen? Why is this happening? What were we doing wrong? We have two kids. One just had knee surgery and couldn't even walk.

To everyone else we must look so irresponsible. What if we are making the worst decision of our lives? What if we've already made the worst decision? We've already sold our house. While we are across town living out of boxes another family is living in our home. For what?

Why had we not just prayed about it before making plans to fly out? Not just pray but actually wait for His response. Why we had not realized the house we molded a scripture around was the one we eliminated before looking at it? Why hadn't we run back to God's path in that moment? We had not only wandered off the path, they had flown off it.

This whole trip had been centered on the house the realtor called about. Which was not even an option. Our finances had not changed on that flight. It wasn't the realtor's fault. His job is to find us houses. Our job as followers was to seek God before moving forward. In our hearts we had our plans already in place before that first phone call ended.

I doubted myself more in those days than I ever had before. My circumstances were consuming me. I needed to come back to God's truth, again. I thought to myself, "How dense could I be?" It seems like every day I wake up and start doing things my way. Completely forgetting that just yesterday my way didn't work. When yesterday I had realized I needed to rely on God and follow His plans. I was learning, the hard way, that everyday my will and my plans needed to cease. I just needed to follow His direction. Every single day I would try to handle things my way and fall on my face. My plans and my will would need to be surrendered daily.

I started repeating to myself constantly. "I believe in God. I believe what He says. I believe His Word is true. I said I would be brave."

We had taken control and lost it again. The only thing we could control was how we handled this. Will we handle it gracefully or not? That decision was up to us.

Ephesians 1:13 And you also were included in Christ when you heard the message of truth, the gospel of your salvation. When you believed, you were marked in him with a seal, the promised Holy Spirit.

Chapter 15

In the last few months I had this nagging feeling to contact churches in east Texas for help finding a house. I repeatedly dismissed the idea. Honestly, it sounded dumb. Who contacts a church to help buy a house? You contact a realtor to buy a house.

At this point in our journey I felt I had nothing to lose. After pulling myself out of my slump I decided to give it a shot. I found a few local churches on social media. Typed up a message and pressed send. I wasn't expecting any replies. We were not exactly in the business of having circumstances work out our way.

I received a message back, less than an hour later. One of the churches had searched through social media pages going back weeks. Pages I had not found through all my hours of striving.

One of the houses stood out to me. Before I even sent it to Bubba I sent a private message to the woman selling it. I had no reason to waste his time if it had already sold.

It was available! That by itself was a miracle considering how long it had been on the market. Everything about the house seemed great, almost too great. Not many photos were listed but based on the description I could see it had everything we needed. Things we were not even expecting. Like the fact it was on two acres. In the beginning of this journey we were looking at ten acres. That expectation had gone out the window a long time ago. All the recent houses sat on less than one acre. Which would have been amazing.

At this point we had no expectations left other than at least three bedrooms. This brick house had three bedrooms. It was near the house Bubba had put an offer on. Significant because this meant he had driven through this neighborhood. The woman that lived in this house with her son felt safe in the neighborhood. This meant it really must be safe.

I had the hardest time trusting the real estate listings that said, "Safe or nice neighborhood." I really believe they are required to say that. A few neighborhoods we had driven in that stated similar things should have stated, "Scary neighborhood, carry a club." The fact that she was living there and felt safe was an answered prayer.

It was amazing to see how thankful we could be when we had practically no expectations. It's crazy how much my perspective had changed from what I could do for myself to what God wanted to do for us. Each detail we learned made this house fit our family more perfectly. I could not have picked a better house had I tried.

The fact that I thought this house seemed great meant practically nothing. I no longer wanted to follow my feelings. My feelings were not to be trusted. I had realized just how easily my feelings were wrong. How often they would lead me astray and off His path.

I sent the link to Bubba. He immediately sent it to the realtor. I tried to control my feelings. I was sure I wouldn't be able to handle another major letdown. We knew if He allowed us to get as far as buying it than this must be the house. The one that God had went ahead of us and prepared. If it wasn't we would start over and keep looking. Within twenty four hours the realtor had plans to see this house.

It was hard to concentrate on anything else knowing he would be calling as soon as he saw it. Feeling like our whole world was going to change when that phone rang. Each time we had received a call or text from him it had been bad news. When he called, we were expecting the worst.

When the call finally came he said this house seemed nicer than the others. We prayed and pursued it. We knew God would close this door if it wasn't the right one. I continued trying to keep my emotions in check. I knew the house being nice had no influence on whether or not this was the house God had prepared for us.

There was a certain detail about the house I couldn't get off my mind, the creek. A small one, but a creek nonetheless. As a child I grew up with a creek. Deep down I had always wanted the same thing for my kids. Never in a million years had I thought it would be possible.

A month later we'd closed on this house. Clearly this was the house God prepared for us. We would step foot into our home for the first time when we arrived in Texas. I'd sit and think about this house and the very bumpy journey to find it. Realizing I was extremely happy God hadn't let us settle for our best.

Leaving the beach was not as hard as I expected. We would miss family, friends, and the church that had prayed us through this whole journey. We couldn't wait to see what God had in store for us. He had a purpose for us and we knew it was going to be amazing.

As we pulled down our new street we were excited to see our home. Rounding the corner our house came into view. It was everything we had wished for. The house was perfect for us. Not too small yet not too big. All the flowers I had left behind were replaced by the most gorgeous rose bushes in full bloom. A Crape Myrtle standing tall in the center of the yard. A large Pampas Grass towering near the mailbox to remind us of the beach.

Was this literally ours! This is what God had in mind the entire time while we had strived and searched. So many times we would have settled for mediocre when His best was just waiting for us.

It was beautiful. It was less than a mile from the hotel we had stayed at in March. Where we had frantically driven hours in all directions searching for the "right" house. How ironic is it that as we stand on the back deck of our home, we can see the house we lost. The house I had wanted so badly. I had been so mad at God for taking that house from me. When all along He had something better in mind. How often do we insist on what we want? Never realizing God can and wants to do so much more for us. Each time I walk out of my back door and see that house it stands as a reminder for me not to push my will. To step back and allow God to lead me. He will and He wants to.

How many tears had I shed striving for what I wanted? How many days had I wasted trying to figure it all out? God knew all along what was going to happen. He knew exactly where we would be. He had listened to the deepest desires of our hearts and wanted all along to fulfill them.

Because of the lessons learned and the faith we now have we will forever be grateful for the pain and heartache that we went through from the beginning of this Journey. We trust Him more now than we ever did before. We know in our hearts that He will come through. That we'd rather have His plan over ours any day. He'd done exactly what He'd said in those scriptures I had prayed over. He would always do what He said. He can be trusted all the time. He can and will provide more than we could ever imagine. We only need to trust Him and wait on Him. He gave us a home we did not strive for. God is good. He will come through for us, every time. God used His people through the church to lead us right to our home. Of course, He would use His church. We are the church.

Psalm 37:4-5 Take delight in the Lord, and
he will give you the desires of your heart.
Commit your way to the Lord; trust in him
and he will do this:

Chapter 16

I felt led to share on social media to keep family and friends informed about our constantly changing journey. I am not a fan of posting my information for everyone to see. This time I was not about to waste anytime obeying His leading. Like I had done when He was leading me to contact the churches.

My obedience was not going to be determined by my feelings or how I thought others would respond. Learning to obey was not for them, it was for me. Reluctantly, I decided to post the updates. I really expected the posts to be filled with photos of fun places and new adventures.

They ended up being filled with struggles and lessons learned. I realized quickly that God was using our struggles to help others. People seemed to relate to what I was saying. They seemed surprised by my candidness. I felt like I was just telling the truth. I knew since God was telling me to do this than He would never tell me to lie. With my personality anything less than the whole truth is a lie. So I shared what was really going on. I shared how I really felt about what was happening.

Included is an update from right after we arrived. Our latest struggle, not knowing where anything was around town or in the surrounding towns. If we needed something at the beach we knew where to go or who to ask. Currently we needed furniture.

This may seem like a completely insignificant problem. To me it was a big problem at the time. We serve a personal God who cares about all our problems whether big or small. To Him they are all significant.

Remember we left or sold most of our belongings. The beach had multiple thrift stores. One we really loved, Dare Challenge Thrift Store. This thrift store benefited a substance abuse ministry. They always had great things for cheap. We loved the cause and the store. We were in search of a similar one. The search for furniture turned into a realization that we weren't from around here. We didn't know anyone or how to find anything. That's an isolating feeling to have.

This post is from August 18, 2018, we had been in east Texas a little over two weeks. *"The house is unpacked! What a relief. Still can't find most of my stuff. That will come with time. We found the thrift store. It's only opened every other Saturday. It's a mall owned by a church. Yes, you read that correctly. Summer Grove Baptist Church bought the mall. The sanctuary is located in one of the stores. The thrift shop located in another. They have beautiful, inexpensive stuff. I'm guessing I'll be there every other Saturday finding every little thing Bubba swears we don't need.*

As we walked out of the thrift shop a lady from the church invited us over to the front doors for a free lunch and school supplies. Everything in me was screaming this isn't for you. You are the server, not the served. All I wanted to do was help them serve people who 'needed' it more. We said, 'No thank you' as we continued walking towards the car. When we arrived at the car, I saw David's face. I could tell exactly what he was thinking. 'Mom, it is lunch time and they want to feed me.'

I tried to think of a reason to explain to him why I was refusing. I couldn't. In his face I saw all the lessons I had learned and taught him. Lessons about how it feels when you are the server and people just walk by and say no. You are trying to explain to them there aren't any strings attached to this gift. How many times I had told him that one of the worst feelings in the world is to organize a ministry to bless people and no one comes. Hearing the wise words of a friend in my head saying, 'Don't take a blessing from someone.' We turned around and started walking to the front doors.

I wish I could say it was easy to walk to those doors. But the truth is, it wasn't. Every step toward that group solidified the fact I didn't have a group or a church to serve with. Just like the many other times I had stepped out of my comfort zone. The actual doing what He said was sometimes the hardest.

No, He did not say audibly to me, 'Go get lunch from them.' But the Holy Spirit did clearly bring to my remembrance the lessons I had learned over the years. Helping me to remember how that lady felt when I said, 'No thank you.'

What a blessing it was. They didn't care that our kids weren't in public school or what county we came from. They were thrilled to be loving on anyone and everyone. Serving Christ no questions asked. Yes, it was weird to walk away and not serve with them. But I needed that reminder of who I was. I'm a server. Always wanting to reach the lost. Seeing the ones on the outskirts. The ones not sure if they are good enough or wanted. I am a missionary. The happiness on their faces to be doing the greatest thing on earth is who and what I am.

They thought they gave us a piece of chicken and some beans. Really it was God reminding us of who and what we are. We are followers of the coolest person in the world, Jesus. When you're serving for the creator of the universe you may think you're serving just beans and chicken. When really you have no idea what part you will play in that person's life who receives it. Beans and chicken may be exactly what they needed that day or just maybe they needed something else you didn't even know you were offering. A reminder of just who God has called them to be."

Through the updates God was showing me how to articulate the lessons He was teaching me. How to use our struggles to glorify Him. The people at the Summer Grove Baptist Church Thrift Shop probably had no idea the impact they had on our family.

Thankfully, through the updates God was showing me how I can testify of His goodness to the people He has placed in my circle of influence.

Just like you can share your struggles and testify of His goodness to your circle. I assure you that you have people around you that

Kelly R. Henley

God has placed there for a purpose. You may be one of the people He uses to encourage them.

We all struggle. We all feel alone in our struggles. Let's continue helping each other and building each other up.

Psalm 71:15 My mouth will tell of your righteous deeds, of your saving acts all day long- though I know not how to relate them all

Chapter 17

We realized just how blessed we were to have learned how to walk in a deeper level of faith. We needed our new trust in God's abilities to continue obeying what He had called us to. Our call to obey, when things were hard, had not ended when we arrived in Texas. Each day we would need to press into God just to keep moving forward.

Bubba had planned for two weeks off work before leaving the beach to visit with family and friends. Plus focus on moving arrangements. And two weeks after arriving to settle in and address anything that may need attention with the house.

When it came time for him to start his new job, through no fault of ours or our friends, there was not a position for him with the company. Circumstances hadn't lined up the way we'd expected.

Thanks to our deeper level of understanding that God would not leave us nor forsake us, we knew this would all work out. Back in our baby faith when we were so, "On fire for God." We were so confident we were ready to go, we weren't. We wouldn't have lasted a day in the life we were living!

Back then we did not have the foundation needed to walk this out. There is a reason why God's timing is not our timing. We would have crumbled without the faith we needed to stand in this uncertainty. To stand and know that God is God. To know God is good even if the situation doesn't look good.

The faith we would need could only come from trials and

experience. At the beginning of our walk we didn't have what it took. God knew it. Thank goodness He doesn't listen to us.

Having faith didn't mean we weren't scared. Bubba had been off work now for over a month. We knew God had a plan. We also knew His plan would be better than what we could come up with on our own. We just needed to follow and wait. We didn't know how or when this would get worked out. But we were determined to handle the uncertainty a little more gracefully this time.

We started to become a little more scared as week after week went on. He applied at place after place only to be turned down. God would lay it on my heart to share an update about the struggles we were going through. I would try to wait until things were better to post.

Remember, the updates were supposed to be great fun updates full of photos of our new adventures. Our adventures now consisted of worrying how we would pay the bills. I was really struggling with the thought of people thinking we had obeyed just to fall on our faces.

He was finally hired at a place. This job would at least pay the bills. He knew it was not where he would stay. He continued praying and following God's leading. With Bubba working every day while using our one vehicle meant the kids and I were left at home in a new town.

I needed people around me. I was determined to not be lonely again. I knew I needed the church. Every week we tried different churches. Knowing God would reveal to us which one was our new church family. We wanted to be exactly where He had chosen for us. We wanted to find the church He had prepared for us.

Finding a church home would prove to be just as emotionally hard for me as finding a house. I need the church in my life. More than I ever knew. After being saved seven years ago, the church was my "thing." The people, the sense of family, and community. I think we were there every chance we got. No one here knew us. We needed a church. I needed a Mom's Group.

We knew He would come through. He always had before. This was just one more time I would need to wait on Him. I couldn't control my circumstances. Although, I could control how fast I let go and let Him lead. I wanted His best, not my best.

Deuteronomy 31:8 "The LORD himself goes before you and will be with you; he will never leave you nor forsake you. Do not be afraid; do not be discouraged."

Chapter 18

A lady approached Bubba while he was out looking for a job one day. She was out of work and looking for assistance. In addition to some money he offered to give her a ride to apply at a few places. He really felt encouraged after praying with her and being able to help her in her need. He realized all he really wanted was a job that provided enough for bills and gave him the ability to serve others.

He received a lead from a company in town. They advised him to head to another business across town that was hiring. He wasn't sure what kind of business it was. At this point any lead was worth checking out.

Later he would learn that a man was sitting at his desk right where he was headed. Praying for God to send the right person for the job. He brought the application home. For some reason he was not planning to return it. Maybe he thought he wasn't qualified. Maybe he wasn't ok with as needed work. He had always been full time. Receiving practically the same number of hours every week for fourteen years. "As needed" lacked the stability we needed. This job also required lots of traveling.

Continuing to pray while pursuing other leads he decides to take that application back. We knew enough about God and about prayer that if we prayed for God to close doors, He would. God would not allow him to get hired if this was not the job for him.

After returning the application he realized a few skills from the cabinet shop would, in fact, benefit him in this position. God had equipped him for this work and they hired him. Having an "as needed" position would require him to trust God to meet our needs. Something that sounds right up God's alley. Traveling for work was something he'd always wanted to do. Telling his grandmother as a boy he wanted to travel when he grew up. This, in our minds, was reserved for when our kids were grown. We realized this was going to be our reality, now.

This job meant lots of experiences and excitement. It also meant he wouldn't be home. Every day since we'd married he'd been home at the same time every day. Now he would be gone often sometimes for a week or longer. There was no denying this job was from God. We had trusted and He had led. As much as we saw God's hand in this it was still very hard. The kids and I were just here alone and without a church.

Not only was Bubba away often but we never knew until the last minute when he would leave or return. I really like to have my plans and my schedules. I really like for them to work out my way. Yet again, we found ourselves with no control over our circumstances. The only thing we had control over was how we responded. We knew with God we could handle anything. God's truth had to become bigger than our feelings. Bigger than our circumstances.

In the moments when I was the most distraught about his job or not having a church there was no denying God was with us. That He had called us here to east Texas. One moment I'd sit in utter shock at the blessings in our lives. In aww of God's love for us. His power to accomplish all this. The next moment I'd feel crushed by my need to control our schedule. My need to know what was going on. My need to know which church was ours.

My need to control. To have my plans work out was what caused me the stress, worry, and problems. It was a battle and it was constant. My emotions would flip flop back and forth hundreds of times a day. Seeking God I would be able to bring my feelings back to the blessings. Remembering the truths I had learned. Being reminded of the example of finding the house just a few months ago. Which had shown me I don't need to have circumstances work my way. I can let go of all my plans and trust God. Trust that He wants what's best for me and my family. Even if I don't understand His plans. His plans are still for my good, always.

Hebrews 13:21 Equip you with everything good for doing his will, and may he work in us what is pleasing to him, through Jesus Christ, to whom be glory forever and ever. Amen

Chapter 19

Before arriving we had researched online many churches in the area. Making a list of all the ones we were excited to try. The larger the internet presence the better. Not because we wanted a big church but a church big into outreach.

Pastor had made it clear to us that we should not judge a church by how updated their website was. "That's crazy. Of course I can judge by a website. We are supposed to reach the lost. And the lost are online too," I thought.

When we first arrived we tried the churches on our list. God made it clear these churches were not in the community He had sent us to. In my heart I knew if He had wanted us in those communities He had been more than capable to send us there. We continued looking online. Realizing judging a church by their website would probably not be effective.

Every Sunday and Wednesday that Bubba was home we tried a new church. I refused to try a new church alone. I did not want my feelings leading us. My feelings were not to be trusted.

We needed a church. My prayers were to hear and see Him. For my feelings to not get in the way. That Bubba would be home on church days. Most of all that it would be clear to us which church He had chosen for us. We were surely getting more confident in our prayers. More confident in knowing God heard us. Knowing that God was always leading us. We needed to be alert. Ready for His direction.

On the church days Bubba wasn't home we would go back

to the churches we had already tried. We knew they weren't our church. But the kids and I had no one. We needed to be around other believers.

They were still great churches full of great believers even if they weren't our church. Although the people were nice, it was hard to walk in over and over and be the new people. I had grown so accustomed to almost everyone knowing us in the church. This was hard, way harder than I expected.

The area around us had more churches than I've ever seen in my life. A whole spread in the newspaper listing them by name and address. It was incredibly overwhelming when searching for a church.

After trying church after church we hung the newspaper on the cross by the door. We started checking them off as we went. God would reveal. We knew He had prepared a way for us. We knew that we could not just pick where we wanted to attend. At this point we didn't want to. We knew that God's choice was the best choice. We wanted His best.

Hebrews 10:25 Not giving up meeting together, as some are in the habit of doing, but encouraging one another-and all the more as you see the Day approaching.

Chapter 20

The kids and I had been waiting to try a church we had researched online. Their website didn't seem to have what we were looking for. Though we had learned a website could not be a deciding factor. God was the deciding factor.

I really wanted to try this church so we contacted them on social media to ask a few questions. We realized they had many activities both kids were excited about. Their website was just outdated. Of course, pastor had been right. I was beginning to see how much I still needed to learn.

We went and all had a great time. God would allow him to be home that following Sunday also. Making it possible for us to try this church's Sunday morning service.

It was exactly the type of church we were looking for. I'll elaborate a bit to help everyone understand what I had been looking for. At this point I was not thinking it was possible. Thinking this kind of church was only possible in bigger cities surely not small towns. Hence the reason the church we first tried had been in a neighboring city. The main thing I had been looking for aside from sound doctrine and values were two sanctuaries. Sounds silly I'm sure.

Keep in mind I am well aware God is not going to just direct me to what I want. I hope our story has made it very clear to you that on many occasions the things I thought I wanted weren't even what was best for me.

What I want in a church shows what is in my heart. I wanted a church that cares more about reaching people than keeping with tradition. Remember all these traditions I have learned in recent years. I feel I have a pretty unique perspective. Helping me to see how very pointless and destructive some traditions can be.

If our goal is to reach the lost and help save souls than we should do everything in our power to relate to the world without compromising our values. We live in a very shallow society. I will admit I can be shallow. Not as shallow as I was when I first started coming to church but still shallow in some ways. I will list a few. I prefer contemporary music to hymns any day. I prefer chairs to pews. For those that may not know what a pew is it's a long bench, sometimes with a cushion. I prefer the light dimmed during worship so I don't feel like people are staring at my face. See, I told you I can be shallow. But so are most people when they are first considering giving the church a chance.

I wanted to be part of a church that was willing to change the traditions to reach the most people. A church that was willing to stop doing what wasn't working anymore. Some traditions may have been great for an earlier generation. Although it's obvious some are not working anymore.

I also know I need more than just those things. I need the Bible to be preached from the pulpit. First and foremost that is the most important criteria for the church to have. God's word is truth. His word is the Bible. Seek God's wisdom while deciding on a church and He will help you. Here is a good scripture to pray when making decisions. James 1:5 If any of you lacks wisdom, you should ask God, who gives generously to all without finding fault, and it will be given to you. Praying over this scripture when I was first saved helped me to discern God's direction. I had no religious background at all and He was still able to direct me. Remember He gives us His wisdom to make the decision.

I need the church to be concerned about families. Families are who changes a community. Which does not just mean focusing on the little kids. If you focus on just the little kids you are sending them home with parents that you did not focus on. Which seems a little unfair to the child. Since it is not the child's job to defend their faith and help save their family. Focusing on families covers the children and their parents. That's the kind of church I wanted to find.

We decided to go back Sunday night for the evening service. As we sat in the service the music director went on stage. He tells a story about moving that weekend. He did not intend to come that night. Therefore, he had not prepared any music for worship. He ended his story with, "After the service this morning God laid it on my heart to play this song."

He begins to play Amazing Grace. Bubba leans over and tells me that during the morning service he had prayed that God would confirm this church to him if it were the one.

As a boy Bubba was very close to his Gram. At her funeral the song Amazing Grace was played. Whenever Bubba needs a confirmation about a direction he will pray for God to show him the way. Usually God's direction comes through this song in some way. To let him know he is on the right track. God knows how to speak right to his heart.

I knew this meant God had confirmed to Bubba that this was our new church. It was nearly impossible to contain myself. I wanted to fall to the floor and cry. I felt my emotions coming up in my chest. I kept telling myself, "Girl, you need to calm down. Cry when you get home." I had been a witness to the many times God had confirmed with this song to know this was for real. This was our church. God doesn't play around. If you ask for specific confirmations and you receive them, it's God. I also knew if I lost it, fell to the floor crying in the middle of the song I'd probably not make any friends.

Our search for a church was over. God is so good. As soon as the service ended Bubba approached the music director. Completely out of character for him. He told him what he'd prayed that morning and the significance.

A man had been standing next to the music director. I didn't know who this man was. But the words this man spoke I will never forget for as long as I live. As he reached his hand out to Bubba he said, "Welcome home."

This was the welcome home I had waited for! God didn't holler it through the clouds but instead used our new brother in Christ to deliver the message to us.

I would later learn this church had a ladies' Bible study group similar to my Mom's Group. This church also had two sanctuaries and wasn't afraid to change things that no longer worked. This church focused on families. They knew the way to change communities was through families. Paying extra attention to reaching the men. Because men lead families. Most of all this church believed in the power of God through His word, the Bible.

Our goal in finding a church had been to have God's best and that's what He gave us. We had set aside our plans and tried our best to focus on Him. Allowing Him full access to lead us. As He led we listened, obeyed, and followed the best we knew how.

Romans 12:2 Do not conform to the pattern of this world but be transformed by the renewing of your mind. Then you will be able to test and approve what God's will is-his good, pleasing and perfect will.

Chapter 21

The church was a perfect fit for everyone in our family except David. Kids don't exactly look for the same qualities in a church that parents do. They look at kid stuff. Are the kids nice and do I fit in? Our son was not feeling like he fit in. He was the only home-schooled kid in his class. Also one of the only kids that didn't play sports.

To me these were insignificant problems. He was the one that didn't want to play sports and at church most kids go to different schools anyway. Although these didn't seem like big problems to me, they were to him. God is a personal God who cares about all our needs. Even if to some they seem small and insignificant.

I knew after talking with him the kids in the class were not making him feel this way. It was his feelings mixed in with a little bit of the enemy's schemes. We prayed and we discussed. Week after week I realized David didn't want to be there. He had always loved being at church as much as I did. We knew God had chosen this church for our family and that meant him too.

I quickly resorted to being upset with God. Why would He have chosen a church that was making our son miserable? Even if it was at no fault of the church. I needed a way for him to fit in.

I received some advice about the area. Funny advice, but probably true nonetheless. "Put David in football. He'll make lots of friends and fit right in." I don't have a football player. I have a boy that likes golf and tennis. Even if he wanted to play football, in this area that's a sport played through public school. "God, this was on you. You caused this so you can fix it," I thought.

One week in particular he was trying to avoid going to Sunday school. Trying to get out of it by hunting with his dad. He had already refused to go along with my idea to bribe his classmates with treats.

"God, he trusts you. He knows you chose this church for our family. You fix this. Lord, help him fit in. Help him make friends. If you can make him fit in with a football player that would be even better."

The next morning they left to hunt. I was surprised when they returned home in enough time to make it to Sunday school. I continued my work in the kitchen while they started telling me about their hunting experience. Honestly, I was only half listening. A hunter's wife can only hear so many deer, squirrel, and raccoon stories before they all sound alike.

Suddenly the story changes. Bubba starts telling me about a note they found on the gate of the hunting property. The note was from a house nearby. Asking them to come by when they were finished hunting. As he tells me the details, it's obvious he was way more interested in the deer part of the story. Although I was hanging onto his every word about this note.

He tells me when he arrived at the house the homeowner simply had a question for him. Asking if he and his son could continue walking through the property to hunt on the adjacent land. Bubba nonchalantly mentions their son is the same age as ours. They also have a daughter the same age as ours and attend the same church as we do. He mentions we should get together with them sometime.

Bubba says the craziest thing as he walks away to change his clothes for church. "Oh, the kid plays football." I was completely shocked and in awe of God's power. Still trying not to show it. Since no one knew I had secretly prayed for God to help our son fit in.

I couldn't hold back my feelings any longer. With tears streaming down my face I prayed, "God, you are so good and so personal." He had heard what I had thought was the dumbest prayer I had ever prayed.

I could not have pulled off what God had pulled off. He was so specific too. A football player in my son's Sunday school class. God's power is amazing. I'm so glad David was more trusting in this than I was. He knew he wanted God to fix this, not mom. He wanted God's best. With that expectation that's exactly what he got.

He also learned some very valuable lessons through this. He learned God cares. God cares about all our needs even if they seem small to others. He also learned he plays a big part in whether he believes the enemy's schemes. By believing he didn't fit in, he had made himself feel even worse. To the point of not wanting to go to church.

Although meeting this family served as an encouragement to us all, God used this situation to help us see that we are missionaries and that's why we fit in. When the creator of the universe tells you to move to a certain town. You start to realize the enemy's schemes are insignificant compared to our direct orders to be in this town. Jesus is why we fit in. No matter how we feel at the time.

2 Corinthians 9:8 And God is able to bless you abundantly, so that in all things at all times, having all that you need, you will abound in every good work.

Chapter 22

Each day this place feels more like home. We have learned there is no place we would rather be than right where God has placed us. He came before us. He prepared this place for us. Most of all He prepared us for this place.

As time passes God meets more and more of our needs through the people here in this little town. We will trust Him when storms come our way. He has proven to us that He is faithful. He is unchanging. Whatever troubles that He allows to come our way are for our good.

We can look back and see each trial had a purpose. Each had a lesson in disguise. God doesn't cause the bad to come on us. Although, He will sometimes allow it and use it for good.

We came here with the assumption that this place and these people needed us. The more time we spend here the more we realize this place didn't need us. We needed this place. We needed these people.

We've learned when God tells us to do something, we will do it. No matter how small and insignificant that it may seem. There are no coincidences. Things don't happen by random chance.

Our story isn't over. We will stumble for sure. More trials will come our way and we will only have control over how we respond. How quickly we let go and let God have control.

God is good and faithful. He will continue to complete in us the work He has begun. And we can't wait.

Post from December 18, 2018 four months after arriving in east

Texas. A song I had been listening to was part of the inspiration for this post. *"Over the last four months I've had so many emotions to work through. Lonely, scared, uncomfortable, anxious, resentful, angry, bitter, and confused to just name a few. All those feelings didn't feel like faith. So I added shame, guilt, and doubt to each one. Emotionally it's been a tough couple of months.*

God was so faithful as I held onto him through each emotion and feeling. He showed me having faith doesn't mean you can't have some of those feelings. Having faith means you choose to trust, choose to believe, and choose to follow Him anyway.

Thinking back to my terrified tears at the beach. Right before we left our home begging, 'God don't do this.' I can't help but remember that small voice that rang louder than my sobs. 'Fear doesn't decide if you follow.'

Each and every moment I've thought I can't take another step He's right there reminding me. 'You aren't alone! Why are you scared and anxious? Not letting go of the beach is making you bitter, resentful, and angry. I'm not confused, why are you?'

The most recent revelation as I sat seeking Him for answers to my emotions was a big, 'Grow up.' All I could do was laugh. 'Yep, got it,' I replied.

That's exactly what I needed to do, grow up. Stop pouting! Stop thinking how things could be different! How things could move faster! I needed to just stop and see how they were. Once I did that everything changed. I saw things through a different perspective. I started to see how much my family loved it here. How much I loved it here.

During a conversation with Nadia on the way home from youth she tells me they asked everyone what they were thankful for in 2018. Her reply floored me. She had answered with, 'Moving here.'

'What? Are you serious? How can that be the thing you're most thankful for? Your parents literally uprooted your entire life! Moved you from everything you've ever known, all your friends, family, and church. To say it's been a rough transition is an understatement. All because God told us to.' Thankfully I only thought that to myself.

Everything in that last statement was fact but not truth. Truth tells us to trust in the Lord with all our heart and lean not on our own understanding. Truth tells us that God's peace surpasses all understanding. Truth tells us that there's no place we would rather be than right where God called us. Everything doesn't have to be going as we want or perfect to have God's peace. Facts say things could be different or better. Truth says there is no place I would rather be. We will trust, we will follow no matter how we feel at the time."

Philippians 4:8 Finally, brothers and sisters, whatever is true, whatever is noble, whatever is right, whatever is pure, whatever is lovely, whatever is admirable- if anything is excellent or praiseworthy- think about such things.

Chapter 23

If you are thinking to yourself I wish I had more honest and caring people in my life. I wish I had more joy and peace. I wish this life had meaning and purpose. I encourage you to open your eyes and look for God's people. They don't know all the answers but they know who does. When you surround yourself with His people you will find what you're looking for. You'll find the people, the joy, and the peace. Along the way you will learn that life has purpose and meaning.

I am in no way saying a life with Jesus is smooth sailing. There are trials. You have read about just a few of ours. With Jesus the bad stuff has a purpose and meaning. He is by our side helping us through it. We are not left to figure it all out ourselves.

I spent twenty seven years of my life lost and didn't know it. I thought life was all about trying to make it work. Make the best out of everything in a messed-up world. Now after seven years with Jesus I can't even fathom how I didn't know I was lost. I was so lost. Everything in my life pointed to how lost I was. Yet, I was oblivious to it.

I saw the churches and assumed those were for different people. I'd see the signs advertising, "All are welcome." I'd think they meant all church people.

Dude, they are talking about you, me, and for real everyone! Literally everyone is welcome! Now that I am what I referred to as a "church person" I can't begin to count how many ways I have tried to explain to people that the church really welcomes everyone. For real, everyone! You don't have to get your life together before you are welcome. You just are. Right now, exactly how you are.

If you feel like you may be missing something in this life. If you find yourself looking to people, material things, and substances for happiness only to realize it only works for a short time. Try the church. Remember the church alone can't save you. But those people know personally the one who can. Just give it a chance. I bet you would try a ten step program to happiness if offered to you. So why not just give Jesus a shot. God will have gone ahead of you and prepared the church for you. Just like He did us.

If you live in an area where people are asking you every day to go with them to church. Just go, try it. They are bugging you because they know something you don't. They know that your life has meaning and purpose. They know you weren't a mistake. They know there is a great plan for your life.

If you live in an area where the church seems like an empty building all week. Just go on Sunday morning. I assure you there will be people there. People who are ready to welcome you into a new family. You are welcome and you are wanted just the way you are. You don't have to know churchy stuff in order to walk in those doors. I didn't. All I knew when I walked in was I wanted more happiness in my life. I didn't want to be lonely anymore. I can confidently say with Jesus and His church in my life I will never be lonely again.

That building may seem empty all week but I promise you it's not. There are church people all around you. When you start seeking Him you'll start to notice Jesus sprinkled everywhere throughout your life. Through the mom down the road, the cashier at the grocery store, and the teacher at your child's school. He has been pursuing you. You just didn't notice. He will provide the support you need to continue learning about Him. Just like He did me.

I did not just wake up one day and have the faith I have now. I slowly grew in my faith by going to church, by going to Bible studies, and surrounding myself with other believers. Looking back the most important factor in my growth was being teachable and being willing to learn from my mistakes.

If you are like me and do not understand things, ask questions. Be willing to ask until you get the answers. The answer will come through God, through His word, and often through His people. James 1:5 If any of you lacks wisdom, you should ask God, who gives generously to all without finding fault, and it will be given to you.

If you are the "church people" and you know what you have. Do not ever stop telling people what you have or inviting them to church. You can't save them but you know who can. Realize that they are looking for you outside of those church doors also. You may be the Christian God uses to show them that they are not alone. You may be the mom down the road, the cashier, or the teacher I was referring to. When we first became Christians simply seeing another Christian was encouraging. Simply seeing their cross necklaces, car bumper stickers, and hearing them talking about Jesus. So sport your Jesus gear and speak of your savior often. You may be exactly the encouragement they needed to take that next step of faith.

The world is telling them they are just a mistake. You know the truth. You know God created them for a great and mighty purpose. You know that before the creation of the universe God chose this time in history for them to be living in your town. When you see that mom struggling to keep a smile in the store, tell her she matters. Tell her He sees her. When you see that troubled teen tell them they are worthy. That He has a plan for them. When you see that man trying to hold it all together, tell him he is enough. He is exactly the man for the task he is faced with. Maybe you are the one He will use to finally get through to them. What a privilege that is.

The world is telling them your building is full of fancy "church people." People that have it all together and have never done anything wrong. It doesn't matter that you know that's not true. What will matter is how you act when that lost person walks in that door. They may not be dressed like you. They may never have opened a Bible; let alone memorized verses like you. They have never attended a Sunday school. They don't know where to sit. *They do not know your church has children's church. They may not even know what children's church even is. So their fidgety toddler is in the seat next to you.*

Our job is to make them feel welcome. Like we've waited all week to see them. Then we invite them back. Faith comes through hearing about Christ. We are to treat others the way Christ has treated us. I know for a fact there was rejoicing in heaven when I accepted Him and when you did! That is how the church should react when new people come, rejoicing. Because their life depends on it.

Ephesians 4:1 As a prisoner for the Lord, then, I urge you to live a life worthy of the calling you have received.

Psalm 139 You have searched me, LORD, and you know me, You know when I sit and when I rise; You perceive my thoughts from afar. You discern my going out and my lying down; you are familiar with all my ways. Before a word is on my tongue you, LORD, know it completely. You hem me in behind and before, and you lay your hand upon me. Such knowledge is too wonderful for me; too lofty for me to attain. Where can I go from your Spirit? Where can I flee from your presence? If I go up to the heavens, you are there; if I make my bed in the depths, you are there. If I rise on the wings of the dawn, if I settle on the far side of the sea, even there your hand will guide me, Your right hand will hold me fast If I say, "surely the darkness will hide me and the light become night around me," even the darkness will not be dark to you; The night will shine like the day, For darkness is as light to you. For you created my inmost being; You knit me together in my mother's womb. I praise you because I am fearfully and wonderfully made; your works are wonderful; I know that full well. My frame was not hidden from you when I was made in the secret place, when I was woven together in the depths of the earth. Your eyes saw my unformed body; all the days ordained for me were written in your book before one of them came to be. How precious to me are your thoughts, God! How vast is the sum of them! Were I to count them, they would outnumber the grains of sand-when I awake, I am still with you. If only you, God, would slay the wicked! Away from me, you who are blood thirsty! They speak of you with evil intent; your adversaries misuse your name. Do I not hate those who hate you, LORD, and abhor those who are in rebellion against you? I have nothing but hatred for them; I count them my enemies. Search me, God, and know my heart; test me and know my anxious thoughts. See if there is any offensive way in me and lead me in the way everlasting.